Comfort Food

Comfort Food

Recipes to soothe, cheer, reassure and indulge

Love Food ® is an imprint of Parragon Books Ltd

Parragon
Queen Street House
4 Queen Street
Bath BA1 IHE, UK

Love Food ® and the accompanying heart device is a trade mark of
Parragon Ltd

Copyright © Parragon Books Ltd 2007

Internal design by Emily Lewis
Cover designed by Jane Bozzard-Hill
Photography by Clive Bozzard-Hill
Home Economy by Sandra Baddeley
Introduction text by Fiona Biggs

ISBN 978-1-4075-4359-8

Printed in China

NOTES FOR THE READER
This book uses metric and imperial measurements. Follow the same
units of measurement throughout; do not mix imperial and metric. All
spoon measurements are level: teaspoons are assumed to be 5 ml and
tablespoons are assumed to be 15 ml. Unless otherwise stated, milk is
assumed to be low fat and eggs are medium-size. The times given are an
approximate guide only. Some recipes contain nuts. If you are allergic
to nuts you should avoid using them and any products containing nuts.

Recipes using raw or very lightly cooked eggs should be avoided by
infants, the elderly, pregnant women, convalescents and anyone
suffering from illness. Pregnant and breast-feeding women are advised
to avoid eating peanuts and peanut products.

CONTENTS

INTRODUCTION

Food that comforts has to be the best food of all. Although food is primarily about nutrition – it is, after all, what keeps you alive – the right kind of food has an amazing power to restore your sense of balance when you're feeling low or when things seem to be getting on top of you. When you're feeling a bit down, or tired, the prospect of your favourite dish can be very comforting – even the very act of cooking it can be enough to start the process of restoring your equilibrium. On the tough days, when you really need some pampering, eating the right dish at the right time is the food equivalent of relaxing in front of the fire in your slippers and dressing gown.

Eating food you've enjoyed on happy occasions, or familiar dishes prepared for you when you were a child, can trigger an emotional response, and will immediately make you feel happier, calmer and more at one with the world. When you're feeling down, or tired, you probably think of the things your mother made for you, and that you will always associate with being loved and cared for. You'll probably find many of these dishes here.

We tend to crave carbohydrate-rich foods when we need comfort – this is because they produce the so-called 'happy' chemicals in the brain that can soothe and relax when we're under pressure or feeling stressed. *Comfort Food* is full of dishes that are not only familiar and warming, but are rich in the complex carbohydrates we need when the going gets tough. The wickedly indulgent desserts may have a little less in terms of nutritional value, but will do your bruised psyche a power of good.

Many of the recipes in this book can be cooked using store-cupboard supplies, with the addition of a few fresh ingredients that can be bought on your way home – so do make sure that you're always well-stocked with flour, sugar, rice for risotto, several kinds of dried pasta, some different types of oil and, of course, chocolate.

SOOTHE

When your nerves are jangling, create a soothing menu from the range of delicious recipes here – perhaps a thick, rich Cream of Chicken Soup, a hearty Thick Beef & Button Onion Casserole, followed by that all-time favourite, Traditional Apple Pie? whichever combination of dishes you choose, you're guaranteed to feel better just thinking about them.

CREAM OF CHICKEN SOUP

SERVES 4

3 tbsp butter

4 shallots, chopped

1 leek, trimmed and sliced

450 g/1 lb skinless chicken breasts,
chopped

600 ml/1 pint chicken stock

1 tbsp chopped fresh parsley

1 tbsp chopped fresh thyme

175 ml/6 fl oz double cream

salt and pepper

sprigs of fresh thyme,
to garnish

fresh crusty rolls,
to serve

Melt the butter in a large saucepan over a medium heat. Add the shallots and cook, stirring, for 3 minutes, until slightly softened. Add the leek and cook for a further 5 minutes, stirring. Add the chicken, stock and herbs, and season with salt and pepper. Bring to the boil, then lower the heat and simmer for 25 minutes, until the chicken is tender and cooked through. Remove from the heat and leave to cool for 10 minutes.

Transfer the soup to a food processor and process until smooth (you may need to do this in batches). Return the soup to the pan and warm over a low heat for 5 minutes.

Stir in the cream and cook for a further 2 minutes, then remove from the heat and ladle into serving bowls. Garnish with sprigs of thyme and serve with fresh crusty rolls.

FRESH TOMATO SOUP

SERVES 4
1 tbsp olive oil
650 g/1 lb 7 oz plum tomatoes
1 onion, cut into quarters
1 garlic clove, sliced thinly
1 celery stick, chopped coarsely
500 ml/18 fl oz vegetable or chicken stock
55 g/2 oz dried anellini or other soup pasta
salt and pepper
fresh flat-leaf parsley, chopped, to garnish

Pour the olive oil into a large, heavy-based saucepan and add the tomatoes, onion, garlic and celery. Cover and cook over a low heat for 45 minutes, occasionally shaking the saucepan gently, until the mixture is pulpy.

Transfer the mixture to a food processor or blender and process to a smooth purée. Push the purée through a sieve into a clean saucepan.

Add the stock and bring to the boil. Add the pasta, bring back to the boil and cook for 8–10 minutes, until the pasta is tender, but still firm to the bite. Season to taste with salt and pepper. Ladle into warmed bowls, sprinkle with the parsley and serve immediately.

PERFECT MASHED POTATO

SERVES 4
900 g/2 lb floury potatoes, such as
King Edward, Maris Piper or Desirée
55 g/2 oz butter, plus extra to serve
3 tbsp hot milk
salt and pepper

Peel the potatoes, placing them in cold water as you do so to prevent them from going brown.

Cut the potatoes into even-sized chunks and cook in a large saucepan of boiling salted water over a medium heat, covered, for 20–25 minutes, until they are tender. Test with the point of a knife, but do make sure you test right to the middle to avoid lumps.

Remove the pan from the heat and drain the potatoes. Return the potatoes to the hot pan and mash with a potato masher until smooth.

Add the butter and continue to mash until it is all mixed in, then add the milk (it is better hot because the potatoes absorb it more quickly to produce a creamier mash).

Taste the mash and season with salt and pepper as necessary. Serve with a knob of butter melted on top.

CAULIFLOWER CHEESE

SERVES 4

1 cauliflower, trimmed and cut into florets
(675 g/1 lb 8 oz prepared weight)
40 g/1½ oz butter
40 g/1½ oz plain flour
450 ml/16 fl oz milk
115 g/4 oz Cheddar cheese, finely grated
whole nutmeg, for grating
salt and pepper
1 tbsp grated Parmesan cheese

Cook the cauliflower in a saucepan of boiling salted water for 4–5 minutes. It should still be firm. Drain, place in a hot 1.4-litre/2½ pint gratin dish and keep warm.

Melt the butter in the rinsed-out saucepan over a medium heat and stir in the flour. Cook for 1 minute, stirring continuously.

Remove from the heat and stir in the milk gradually until you have a smooth consistency.

Return to a low heat and continue to stir while the sauce comes to the boil and thickens. Reduce the heat and simmer gently, stirring constantly, for about 3 minutes until the sauce is creamy and smooth.

Remove from the heat and stir in the Cheddar cheese and a good grating of the nutmeg. Taste and season well with salt and pepper.

Pour the hot sauce over the cauliflower, top with the Parmesan cheese and place under a hot grill to brown. Serve immediately.

SHEPHERD'S PIE

SERVES 4

*900 g/2 lb floury potatoes, such as
King Edward, Maris Piper or Desirée*
350 g/12 oz cold roast lamb, minced
1 onion, finely chopped
2 tbsp plain flour
1 tbsp tomato purée
300 ml/10 fl oz vegetable stock
2 tbsp chopped fresh parsley
4 tbsp milk
25 g/1 oz butter
salt and pepper

Preheat the oven to 180°C/350°F/Gas Mark 4.

Peel the potatoes and cut them into chunks. Cook in a large saucepan of lightly salted water for 15 minutes, or until tender.

Meanwhile, put the lamb, onion, flour, tomato purée, stock, parsley and salt and pepper to taste in a bowl and mix together. Turn out the mixture into an ovenproof dish.

Drain the cooked potatoes, then mash in the saucepan until smooth. Over a low heat, beat in the milk, butter and salt and pepper to taste until well mixed. Spoon on top of the lamb. Mark the top with a fork.

Bake in the oven for 30 minutes, or until golden brown. Serve immediately.

THICK BEEF & BUTTON

ONION CASSEROLE

SERVES 6

2 tbsp olive oil

450 g/1 lb button onions, peeled but kept whole

2 garlic cloves, halved

900 g/2 lb stewing beef, cubed

½ tsp ground cinnamon

1 tsp ground cloves

1 tsp ground cumin

2 tbsp tomato purée

750 ml/22 fl oz full-bodied red wine

grated rind and juice of 1 orange

1 bay leaf

salt and pepper

1 tbsp chopped fresh flat-leaf parsley, to garnish

Preheat the oven to 150°C/300°F/Gas Mark 2. Heat the oil in a large, flameproof casserole and cook the whole onions and garlic, stirring frequently, for 5 minutes, or until softened and beginning to brown. Add the beef and cook over a high heat, stirring frequently, for 5 minutes, or until browned on all sides and sealed.

Stir the spices and tomato purée into the casserole and add salt and pepper to taste. Pour in the wine, scraping any sediment from the base of the casserole, then add the orange rind and juice and the bay leaf. Bring to the boil and cover.

Cook in the preheated oven for about 1¼ hours. Remove the lid and cook the casserole for a further hour, stirring once or twice, until the meat is tender. Remove from the oven, garnish with the parsley and serve hot.

ROAST CHICKEN

SERVES 6

1 free-range chicken, weighing 2.25 kg/5 lb
55 g/2 oz butter
2 tbsp chopped fresh lemon thyme
1 lemon, quartered
125 ml/4 fl oz white wine
salt and pepper
roast potatoes and lemon wedges, to serve
6 fresh thyme sprigs, to garnish

Preheat the oven to 220°C/425°F/Gas Mark 7. Make sure the chicken is clean, wiping it inside and out using kitchen paper, and place in a roasting tin.

Place the butter in a bowl and soften with a fork, then mix in the thyme and season well with salt and pepper. Butter the chicken all over with the herb butter, inside and out, and place the lemon quarters inside the body cavity. Pour the wine over the chicken.

Roast the chicken in the centre of the oven for 20 minutes. Reduce the temperature to 190°C/375°F/Gas Mark 5 and continue to roast for a further 1¼ hours, basting frequently. Cover with foil if the skin begins to brown too much. If the tin dries out, add a little more wine or water.

Test that the chicken is cooked by piercing the thickest part of the leg with a sharp knife or skewer and making sure the juices run clear. Remove from the oven.

Remove the chicken from the roasting tin and place on a warmed serving plate to rest, covered with foil, for 10 minutes before carving.

Place the roasting tin on the top of the hob and bubble the pan juices gently over a low heat until they have reduced and are thick and glossy. Season to taste with salt and pepper.

Serve the chicken with the pan juices, roast potatoes and lemon wedges and scatter with the thyme sprigs.

CHOCOLATE CHIP ICE CREAM WITH

HOT CHOCOLATE FUDGE SAUCE

SERVES 4–6

300 ml/10 fl oz full-fat milk

1 vanilla pod

85 g/3 oz caster sugar

3 egg yolks

300 ml/10 fl oz whipping cream

115 g/4 oz milk chocolate,
chopped into small pieces

CHOCOLATE FUDGE SAUCE

50 g/1¾ oz milk chocolate,
broken into pieces

25 g/1 oz butter

4 tbsp full-fat milk

225 g/8 oz soft light brown sugar

2 tbsp golden syrup

Pour the milk into a heavy-based saucepan, add the vanilla pod and bring almost to the boil. Remove from the heat and leave to infuse for 30 minutes.

Put the sugar and egg yolks in a large bowl and whisk together until pale and the mixture leaves a trail when the whisk is lifted. Remove the vanilla pod from the milk, then slowly add the milk to the sugar mixture, stirring all the time with a wooden spoon. Strain the mixture into the rinsed-out saucepan or a double boiler and cook over a low heat for 10–15 minutes, stirring all the time, until the mixture thickens enough to coat the back of the spoon. Do not boil or it will curdle. Remove the custard from the heat and leave to cool for at least 1 hour, stirring from time to time to prevent a skin from forming. Meanwhile, whip the cream until it holds its shape. Keep in the refrigerator until ready to use.

If using an ice cream machine, fold the cold custard into the whipped cream, then churn the mixture in the machine following the manufacturer's instructions. Just before the ice cream freezes, add the chocolate pieces. Alternatively, freeze the custard in a freezerproof container, uncovered, for 1–2 hours, or until it begins to set around the edges. Turn the custard into a bowl and stir with a fork or beat in a food processor until smooth. Fold in the whipped cream and chocolate pieces. Return to the freezer and freeze for a further 2–3 hours, or until firm or required. Cover the container with a lid for storing.

Make the chocolate fudge sauce just before you serve the ice cream. Put the chocolate, butter and milk in a heatproof bowl set over a saucepan of simmering water and heat gently, stirring occasionally, until the chocolate has melted and the sauce is smooth. Transfer the mixture to a heavy-based saucepan and stir in the sugar and syrup. Heat gently until the sugar has dissolved, then bring to the boil and boil, without stirring, for 5 minutes. Serve the hot sauce poured over the ice cream.

TRADITIONAL APPLE PIE

SERVES 6

PASTRY

350 g/12 oz plain flour

pinch of salt

85 g/3 oz butter or margarine, cut into small pieces

85 g/3 oz lard or white vegetable fat, cut into small pieces

about 6 tbsp cold water

beaten egg or milk, for glazing

FILLING

750 g–1 kg/1 lb 10 oz–2 lb 4 oz cooking apples, peeled, cored and sliced

125 g/4¹/₂ oz soft light brown or caster sugar, plus extra for sprinkling

¹/₂–1 tsp ground cinnamon, mixed spice or ground ginger

1–2 tbsp water (optional)

To make the pastry, sift the flour and salt into a mixing bowl. Add the butter and fat and rub in with the fingertips until the mixture resembles fine breadcrumbs. Add the water and gather the mixture together into a dough. Wrap the dough and chill in the refrigerator for 30 minutes.

Preheat the oven to 220°C/425°F/Gas Mark 7. Roll out almost two-thirds of the pastry thinly and use to line a deep 23-cm/9-inch pie plate or pie tin.

Mix the apples with the sugar and spice and pack into the pastry case; the filling can come up above the rim. Add the water if needed, particularly if the apples are not very juicy.

Roll out the remaining pastry to form a lid. Dampen the edges of the pie rim with water and position the lid, pressing the edges firmly together. Trim and crimp the edges.

Using the trimmings, cut out leaves or other shapes to decorate the top of the pie; dampen and attach. Glaze the top of the pie with beaten egg or milk, make 1 or 2 slits in the top and place the pie on a baking sheet.

Bake in the preheated oven for 20 minutes, then reduce the temperature to 180°C/350°F/Gas Mark 4 and bake for a further 30 minutes, or until the pastry is a light golden brown. Serve hot or cold, sprinkled with sugar.

TIRAMISU

SERVES 4

200 ml/7 fl oz strong black coffee, cooled

to room temperature

4 tbsp orange-flavoured liqueur,

such as Cointreau

3 tbsp orange juice

16 Italian sponge fingers

250 g/9 oz mascarpone cheese

300 ml/10 fl oz double cream, lightly whipped

3 tbsp icing sugar

grated rind of 1 orange

60 g/2¹/₄ oz chocolate, grated

TO DECORATE

chopped toasted almonds

crystallized orange peel

Pour the cooled coffee into a jug and stir in the liqueur and orange juice. Put 8 of the sponge fingers in the bottom of a serving dish, then pour over half the coffee mixture.

Put the mascarpone cheese in a separate bowl with the cream, sugar and orange rind and mix together well. Spread half the mascarpone mixture over the coffee-soaked sponge fingers, then arrange the remaining sponge fingers on top. Pour over the remaining coffee mixture and then spread over the remaining mascarpone mixture. Scatter over the chocolate, cover and chill in the refrigerator for at least 2 hours.

Serve decorated with chopped toasted almonds and crystallized orange peel.

CHEER

Had a bad day at the office? Feel as if nothing's going right? Have a look at what's on offer here to create the perfect cheering-up menu. Try traditional Fish & Chips or Macaroni & Seafood Bake, and round the meal off with a super-indulgent helping of wicked Mississippi Mud Pie.

FISH & CHIPS

SERVES 2

vegetable oil, for deep-frying

3 large potatoes, such as Cara or Desirée

2 thick cod or haddock fillets,
175 g/6 oz each

175 g/6 oz self-raising flour, plus extra
for dusting

200 ml/7 fl oz cold lager

salt and pepper

lemon wedges, to garnish

Heat the oil in a temperature-controlled deep-fat fryer to 120°C/250°F, or in a heavy-based saucepan, checking the temperature with a thermometer, to blanch the chips. Preheat the oven to 150°C/300°F/Gas Mark 2.

Peel the potatoes and cut into even-sized chips. Fry for 8–10 minutes, depending on size, until softened but not coloured. Remove from the oil, drain on kitchen paper and place in a warm dish in the warm oven. Increase the temperature of the oil to 180–190°C/350–375°F, or until a cube of bread browns in 30 seconds.

Meanwhile, season the fish with salt and pepper to taste and dust it lightly with a little flour.

Make a thick batter by sifting the flour into a bowl with a little salt and whisking in most of the lager. Check the consistency before adding the remainder: it should be very thick, like double cream.

Dip one fillet into the batter and allow the batter to coat it thickly. Carefully place the fish in the hot oil, then repeat with the other fillet. Cook for 8–10 minutes, depending on the thickness of the fish. Turn the fillets over halfway through the cooking time. Remove the fish from the fryer or saucepan, drain and keep warm.

Make sure the oil temperature is still at 180°C/350°F and return the chips to the fryer or saucepan. Cook for a further 2–3 minutes until golden brown and crispy. Drain and season with salt and pepper before serving with the battered fish, garnished with lemon wedges.

PIZZA

SERVES 2

PIZZA BASE

225 g/8 oz strong white bread flour, plus extra
for dusting
1 tsp easy-blend dried yeast
1 tsp salt
2 tbsp olive oil
225–350 ml/8–12 fl oz warm water

TOPPING

4 tbsp olive oil
1 large onion, thinly sliced
6 button mushrooms, thinly sliced
¹/₂ small green pepper, ¹/₂ small red pepper and ¹/₂ small
yellow pepper, deseeded and thinly sliced
300 g/10¹/₂ oz ready-made tomato pasta sauce
55 g/2 oz mozzarella cheese, thickly sliced
2 tbsp freshly grated Parmesan cheese
1 tsp chopped fresh basil

Combine the flour, yeast and salt in a mixing bowl. Drizzle over half the oil. Make a well in the centre and pour in the water. Mix to a firm dough and shape into a ball. Turn out onto a floured work surface and knead until it is no longer sticky. Oil the bowl with the remaining oil. Put the dough in the bowl and turn to coat with oil. Cover with a tea towel and leave to rise for 1 hour.

When the dough has doubled in size, punch it down to release the excess air, then knead until smooth. Divide in half and roll into 2 thin rounds. Place on a metal tray or baking sheet.

Preheat the oven to 220°C/425°F/Gas Mark 7. For the topping, heat the oil in a frying-pan and cook the vegetables for 5 minutes or until softened. Spread some of the tomato sauce over the pizza bases, but do not go right to the edge. Top with the vegetables and mozzarella cheese. Spoon over more tomato sauce, then sprinkle with Parmesan cheese and chopped basil. Bake for 10 minutes, or until the base is crispy and the cheese has melted.

BURGER & CHIPS

SERVES 4
750 g/1 lb 10 oz fresh beef mince
1 beef stock cube
1 tbsp minced dried onion
2 tbsp water
55 g/2 oz grated Cheddar cheese (optional)
4 sesame buns, toasted
tomato ketchup
large tomato, sliced
lettuce leaves
chips (optional)

Place the beef in a large mixing bowl. Crumble the stock cube over the meat, add the dried onion and water and mix well. Divide the meat into 4 portions, shape each into a ball, then flatten slightly to make a burger shape of your preferred thickness.

Preheat a griddle over a high heat. Place the burgers on the griddle and cook for about 5 minutes on each side, depending on how well done you like your meat and the thickness of the burgers. Press down occasionally with a spatula or palette knife during cooking.

To make cheeseburgers, sprinkle the cheese on top of the meat when you have turned it the first time.

Serve the burgers on toasted buns, with tomato ketchup, sliced tomatoes, lettuce and chips, if liked.

MACARONI & SEAFOOD BAKE

SERVES 4

350 g/12 oz dried short-cut macaroni

85 g/3 oz butter, plus extra for greasing

2 small fennel bulbs, thinly sliced

175 g/6 oz mushrooms, thinly sliced

175 g/6 oz cooked peeled prawns

pinch of cayenne pepper

300 ml/10 fl oz Béchamel sauce

55 g/2 oz freshly grated Parmesan cheese

2 large tomatoes, sliced

olive oil, for brushing

1 tsp dried oregano

salt and pepper

Preheat the oven to 180°C/350°F/Gas Mark 4. Bring a large saucepan of lightly salted water to the boil. Add the pasta, return to the boil and cook for 8–10 minutes, or until tender but still firm to the bite. Drain and return to the saucepan. Add 25 g/1 oz of the butter to the pasta, cover, shake the saucepan and keep warm.

Melt the remaining butter in a separate saucepan. Add the fennel and fry for 3–4 minutes. Stir in the mushrooms and fry for a further 2 minutes. Stir in the prawns, then remove the saucepan from the heat.

Stir the cayenne pepper into the Béchamel sauce and add the prawn mixture and pasta.

Grease a large ovenproof dish with butter, then pour the mixture into the dish and spread evenly. Sprinkle over the Parmesan cheese and arrange the tomato slices in a ring around the edge. Brush the tomatoes with olive oil, then sprinkle over the oregano and season to taste. Bake in the preheated oven for 25 minutes, or until golden brown. Serve immediately.

NACHOS

SERVES 6

175 g/6 oz tortilla chips

400 g/14 oz canned refried beans, warmed

2 tbsp finely chopped bottled jalapeño chillies

200 g/7 oz canned or bottled pimientos
or roasted peppers, drained and finely sliced

115 g/4 oz Gruyère cheese, grated

115 g/4 oz Cheddar cheese, grated

salt and pepper

guacamole and soured cream, to serve

Preheat the oven to 200°C/400°F/Gas Mark 6.

Spread the tortilla chips out over the base of a large, shallow ovenproof dish or roasting tin. Cover with the warmed refried beans. Sprinkle over the chillies and pimientos and season to taste with salt and pepper. Mix the cheeses together in a bowl and sprinkle on top.

Bake in the oven for 5–8 minutes until the cheese is bubbling and melted. Serve immediately with some guacamole and soured cream.

PERFECT ROAST POTATOES

SERVES 6

*1.3 kg/3 lb large floury potatoes, such as
King Edward, Maris Piper or Desirée, peeled
and cut into even-sized chunks*

salt

3 tbsp dripping, goose fat, duck fat or olive oil

Preheat the oven to 220°C/425°F/Gas Mark 7.

Cook the potatoes in a large saucepan of lightly salted boiling water over a medium heat, covered, for 5–7 minutes. They will still be firm. Remove from the heat. Meanwhile, add the fat to a roasting tin and place in the hot oven.

Drain the potatoes well and return them to the saucepan. Cover with the lid and firmly shake the pan so that the surface of the potatoes is slightly roughened to help give a much crisper texture.

Remove the roasting tin from the oven and carefully tip the potatoes into the hot fat. Baste them to ensure that they are all coated with it.

Roast the potatoes at the top of the oven for 45–50 minutes or until they are browned all over and thoroughly crisp. Turn the potatoes and baste again only once during the process or the crunchy edges will be destroyed.

Using a slotted spoon, carefully transfer the potatoes from the roasting tin into a warmed serving dish. Sprinkle with a little salt and serve immediately. Any leftovers (although this is most unlikely) are delicious cold.

CHOCOLATE CHIP BISCUITS

MAKES 18

215 g/7½ oz plain flour, sifted

1 tsp baking powder

115 g/4 oz soft margarine

125 g/4½ oz light brown sugar

50 g/1¾ oz caster sugar

½ tsp vanilla essence

1 egg

115 g/4 oz plain dark chocolate chips

Preheat the oven to 190°C/375°F/Gas Mark 5. Place all the ingredients in a large mixing bowl and beat until they are thoroughly combined.

Lightly grease 2 baking sheets. Place 9 tablespoonfuls of the mixture onto each baking sheet, spacing them well apart to allow for spreading during cooking.

Bake in the oven for 10–12 minutes until the biscuits are golden brown. Using a spatula, transfer the biscuits to a wire rack to cool completely before serving.

FRENCH TOAST WITH MAPLE SYRUP

SERVES 4–6

6 eggs

175 ml/6 fl oz milk

¼ tsp ground cinnamon

salt

*12 slices day-old challah or plain
white bread*

about 4 tbsp butter or margarine, plus extra to serve

½ –1 tbsp sunflower or corn oil

warm maple syrup, to serve

Preheat the oven to 140°C/275°F/Gas Mark 1. Break the eggs into a large, shallow bowl and beat together with the milk, cinnamon and salt to taste. Add the bread slices and press them down so that they are covered on both sides with the egg mixture. Leave the bread to stand for 1–2 minutes to soak up the egg mixture, turning the slices over once.

Melt half the butter with ½ tablespoon of oil in a large frying pan. Add as many bread slices as will fit in a single layer to the pan and cook for 2–3 minutes until golden brown.

Turn the bread slices over and cook until golden brown on the other side. Transfer the French toast to a plate and keep warm in the oven while cooking the remaining bread slices, adding extra oil if necessary.

Serve the French toast with the remaining butter melting on top and warm maple syrup for pouring over.

GINGERBREAD SQUARES

MAKES 24

90 g/3¹/₄ oz butter or margarine, plus extra for greasing

55 g/2 oz muscovado sugar

5 tbsp black treacle

1 egg white

1 tsp almond essence

175 g/6 oz plain flour, plus extra for dusting

¹/₄ tsp bicarbonate of soda

¹/₄ tsp baking powder

pinch of salt

¹/₂ tsp mixed spice

¹/₂ tsp ground ginger

125 g/4¹/₂ oz dessert apples, cooked and finely chopped

Preheat the oven to 180°C/350°F/Gas Mark 4. Grease a large baking tray and line it with baking paper. Put the butter, sugar, treacle, egg white and almond essence into a food processor and blend until smooth.

In a separate bowl, sift the flour, bicarbonate of soda, baking powder, salt, mixed spice and ginger together. Add to the creamed mixture and beat together thoroughly. Stir in the chopped apples. Pour the mixture onto the prepared baking tray.

Transfer to the oven and bake for 10 minutes, or until golden brown. Remove from the oven and cut into 24 pieces. Transfer the squares to a wire rack and let them cool completely before serving.

MISSISSIPPI MUD PIE

SERVES 12–14

CRUMB CRUST

140 g/5 oz digestive biscuits

85 g/3 oz pecans, finely chopped

1 tbsp light brown sugar

½ tsp ground cinnamon

85 g/3 oz butter, melted

FILLING

225 g/8 oz butter or margarine, plus extra for greasing

175 g/6 oz plain dark chocolate, chopped

125 ml/4 fl oz golden syrup

4 large eggs, beaten

85 g/3 oz pecans, finely chopped

Preheat the oven to 180°C/350°F/Gas Mark 4. Lightly grease a 23-cm/9-inch springform or loose-based cake tin.

To make the crumb crust, put the digestive biscuits, pecans, sugar and cinnamon into a food processor and process until fine crumbs form – do not overprocess to a powder. Add the melted butter and process again until moistened.

Tip the crumb mixture into the cake tin and press over the base and about 4 cm/1½ inches up the side of the tin. Cover the tin and chill while making the filling.

To make the filling, put the butter, chocolate and golden syrup into a saucepan over a low heat and stir until melted and blended. Leave to cool, then beat in the eggs and pecans.

Pour the filling into the chilled crumb crust and smooth the surface. Bake in the oven for 30 minutes, or until just set but still soft in the centre. Leave to cool on a wire rack. Serve at room temperature or chilled.

REASSURE

Sometimes you just need to restore the feeling that all's right with the world. The best way to do that is by creating a menu that includes some of your favourite and most familiar recipes – Leek & Potato Soup, Pot-Roasted Leg of Lamb served with Home-made Oven Chips, finished off with some richer than rich Chocolate Fudge Cake.

LEEK & POTATO SOUP

SERVES 4–6
55 g/2 oz butter
1 onion, chopped
3 leeks, sliced
225 g/8 oz potatoes, peeled and
cut into 2-cm/³⁄₄-inch cubes
850 ml/1½ pints vegetable stock
salt and pepper
150 ml/5 fl oz single cream (optional)
flat-leaf parsley, to garnish
crusty bread, to serve

Melt the butter in a large saucepan over a medium heat, add the prepared vegetables and sauté gently for 2–3 minutes until soft but not brown. Pour in the stock, bring to the boil, then reduce the heat and simmer, covered, for 15 minutes.

Remove from the heat and liquidize the soup in the saucepan using a hand-held stick blender if you have one. Otherwise, pour into a blender, liquidize until smooth and return to the rinsed-out saucepan.

Heat the soup, season with salt and pepper to taste and serve in warm bowls. Swirl with the cream, if using, garnish with flat-leaf parsley and serve with crusty bread.

ASPARAGUS & GORGONZOLA

PASTA SAUCE WITH CREAM

SERVES 4
450 g/1 lb asparagus tips
olive oil
salt and pepper
225 g/8 oz Gorgonzola, crumbled
175 ml/6 fl oz double cream
350 g/12 oz dried penne

Preheat the oven to 230°C/450°F/Gas Mark 8.

Place the asparagus tips in a single layer in a shallow ovenproof dish. Sprinkle with a little olive oil. Season with salt and pepper. Turn to coat in the oil and seasoning.

Roast the asparagus in the preheated oven for 10–12 minutes until slightly browned and just tender. Set aside and keep warm.

Combine the crumbled cheese with the cream in a bowl. Season with salt and pepper.

Cook the pasta in plenty of boiling salted water until al dente. Drain and transfer to a warm serving dish.

Immediately add the asparagus and the cheese mixture. Toss well until the cheese has melted and the pasta is coated with the sauce. Serve at once.

HOME-MADE OVEN CHIPS

SERVES 4
450 g/1 lb potatoes
2 tbsp sunflower oil
salt and pepper

Preheat the oven to 200°C/400°F/Gas Mark 6.

Cut the potatoes into thick, even-sized chips. Rinse them under cold running water and then dry well on a clean tea towel. Put in a bowl, add the oil and toss together until coated.

Spread the chips on a baking sheet and cook in the oven for 40–45 minutes, turning once, until golden. Add salt and pepper to taste and serve hot.

RISOTTO

SERVES 4

2 litres/3¹/₂ pints stock or water

1 tbsp olive oil

3 tbsp butter

1 small onion, finely chopped

450 g/1 lb arborio rice

salt and pepper

55 g/2 oz freshly grated Parmesan cheese or Grana Padano, plus shavings to garnish

Bring the stock to the boil, then reduce the heat and keep simmering gently over a low heat while you are cooking the risotto. Heat the oil with 2 tablespoons of the butter in a deep saucepan over a medium heat until the butter has melted. Stir in the onion and cook gently until soft and starting to turn golden. Do not brown.

Add the rice and mix to coat in the oil and butter. Cook and stir for 2–3 minutes, or until the grains are translucent. Gradually add the stock, a ladle at a time. Stir constantly and add more liquid as the rice absorbs it. Increase the heat to moderate so that the liquid bubbles. Cook for 20 minutes, or until all the liquid is absorbed. Season to taste with salt and pepper but don't add too much salt as the Parmesan cheese is salty. The risotto should be of a creamy consistency with a bit of bite in the rice.

Remove the risotto from the heat and add the remaining butter. Mix well, then stir in the Parmesan cheese until it melts. Taste and adjust the seasoning, then serve, garnished with Parmesan cheese shavings.

TORTILLA ESPAÑOLA

SERVES 8 AS PART OF A TAPAS MEAL
250 ml/9 fl oz Spanish olive oil
450 g/1 lb waxy potatoes, peeled and
cut into small cubes or wedges
2 onions, chopped
2 large eggs
salt and pepper

Heat the olive oil in a large, heavy-based or non-stick frying pan. Add the potato pieces and onions, then reduce the heat and fry the potatoes, stirring frequently so that they do not clump together, for 20 minutes, or until they are tender but not browned.

Meanwhile, beat the eggs lightly in a large bowl and season well with salt and pepper. Place a sieve over a large bowl. When the potatoes and onions are cooked, drain them into the sieve so that the bowl catches the oil. Reserve the oil. When drained, gently stir the potatoes and onions into the beaten eggs.

Wipe the frying pan clean or wash it if necessary to prevent the tortilla from sticking. Heat 2 tablespoons of the reserved olive oil in the pan. When hot, add the egg and potato mixture, reduce the heat and cook for 3–5 minutes, or until the underside is just set. Use a spatula to push the potatoes down into the egg so that they are completely submerged, and keep loosening the tortilla from the base of the pan to stop it sticking.

To cook the second side of the tortilla, cover it with a plate and hold the plate in place with your hand. Drain off the oil from the pan, then quickly turn the pan upside down so that the tortilla falls onto the plate. Return the frying pan to the heat and add a little more of the reserved oil to it if necessary. Slide the tortilla, cooked side uppermost, back into the pan and fry for a further 3–5 minutes, or until set underneath. The tortilla is cooked when it is firm and crisp on the outside but still slightly runny in the centre.

Slide the tortilla onto a serving plate and leave to stand for about 15 minutes. Serve it warm or cold.

CHILLI CON CARNE

SERVES 6

2 tbsp corn oil

2 onions, chopped

1 garlic clove, chopped

1 tbsp plain flour

salt and pepper

900 g/2 lb braising steak, diced

300 ml/10 fl oz beef stock

300 ml/10 fl oz red wine

2–3 fresh red chillies, deseeded and chopped

800 g/1 lb 12 oz canned red kidney beans, drained and rinsed

400 g/14 oz canned tomatoes

tortilla chips, to serve

Heat half of the oil in a heavy-based saucepan. Add half the chopped onion and the garlic and cook, stirring occasionally, for 5 minutes, until softened. Remove with a slotted spoon.

Place the flour on a plate and season, then toss the meat in the flour to coat. Cook the meat, in batches, until browned all over, then return the meat and onion to the saucepan. Pour in the stock and wine and bring to the boil, stirring. Reduce the heat and simmer for 1 hour.

Meanwhile, heat the remaining oil in a frying pan. Add the remaining onion and the red chillies and cook, stirring occasionally, for 5 minutes. Add the beans and tomatoes with their juice and break up with a wooden spoon. Simmer for 25 minutes, until thickened.

Divide the meat between individual plates and top with the bean mixture. Serve with tortilla chips.

POT-ROASTED LEG OF LAMB

SERVES 4

1 leg of lamb, weighing 1.6 kg/3 lb 8 oz

salt and pepper

3–4 fresh rosemary sprigs

115 g/4 oz streaky bacon rashers

4 tbsp olive oil

2–3 garlic cloves, crushed

2 onions, sliced

2 carrots, sliced

2 celery sticks, sliced

300 ml/10 fl oz dry white wine

1 tbsp tomato purée

300 ml/10 fl oz lamb or chicken stock

3 medium tomatoes, peeled, quartered
and deseeded

1 tbsp chopped fresh parsley

1 tbsp chopped fresh oregano or marjoram

fresh rosemary sprigs, to garnish

Wipe the lamb all over with kitchen paper, trim off any excess fat and season to taste with salt and pepper, rubbing well in. Lay the sprigs of rosemary over the lamb, cover evenly with the bacon rashers and tie securely in place with kitchen string.

Heat the oil in a frying pan and fry the lamb over a medium heat for 10 minutes, turning several times. Remove from the pan.

Preheat the oven to 160°C/325°F/Gas Mark 3. Transfer the oil from the frying pan to a large flameproof casserole and cook the garlic and onions for 3–4 minutes until the onions are beginning to soften. Add the carrots and celery and cook for a further few minutes.

Lay the lamb on top of the vegetables and press down to partly submerge. Pour the wine over the lamb, add the tomato purée and simmer for 3–4 minutes. Add the stock, tomatoes and herbs and season to taste with salt and pepper. Return to the boil for a further 3–4 minutes.

Cover the casserole tightly and cook in the oven for 2–2¹/₂ hours until very tender.

Remove the lamb from the casserole and, if you like, remove the bacon and herbs together with the string. Keep the lamb warm. Strain the juices, skimming off any excess fat, and serve in a jug. The vegetables may be put around the joint or in a dish. Garnish with sprigs of rosemary.

CHOCOLATE FUDGE CAKE

SERVES 8

175 g/6 oz unsalted butter, softened,
plus extra for greasing
175 g/6 oz golden caster sugar
3 eggs, beaten
3 tbsp golden syrup
40 g/1½ oz ground almonds
175 g/6 oz self-raising flour
pinch of salt
40 g/1½ oz cocoa powder

ICING

225 g/8 oz plain chocolate,
broken into pieces
55 g/2 oz dark muscovado sugar
225 g/8 oz unsalted butter, diced
5 tbsp evaporated milk
½ tsp vanilla essence

Grease and line the base of 2 x 20-cm/8-inch cake tins. To make the icing, place the chocolate, sugar, butter, evaporated milk and vanilla essence in a heavy-based saucepan. Heat gently, stirring constantly, until melted. Pour into a bowl and leave to cool. Cover and chill in the refrigerator for 1 hour, or until spreadable.

Preheat the oven to 180°C/350°F/Gas Mark 4. Place the butter and sugar in a bowl and beat together until light and fluffy. Gradually beat in the eggs. Stir in the syrup and ground almonds. Sift the flour, salt and cocoa powder into a separate bowl, then fold into the mixture. Add a little water, if necessary, to make a dropping consistency. Spoon the mixture into the prepared tins and bake in the oven for 30–35 minutes, or until they are springy to the touch and a skewer inserted in the centre comes out clean.

Leave the cakes in the tins for 5 minutes, then turn out onto wire racks to cool completely. When the cakes are cold, sandwich them together with half the icing. Spread the remaining icing over the top and sides of the cake, cut into wedges and serve.

BUTTER PECAN ICE CREAM

SERVES 8–10

350 ml/12 fl oz double cream
175 ml/6 fl oz milk
6 egg yolks
50 g/1³/₄ oz caster sugar
115 g/4 oz cooled clarified butter
225 g/8 oz roughly chopped pecans

Bring 125 ml/4 fl oz of the cream and all the milk to the boil in a saucepan over a medium-high heat. Remove the saucepan from the heat and leave the mixture to cool completely. Pour into a bowl, cover and leave to chill for 30 minutes.

Using an electric mixer on high speed, beat the egg yolks with 4 tablespoons of the sugar until pale and thick enough to hold a ribbon on the surface when the beaters are lifted. Reserve until required.

Combine the remaining cream and sugar in the rinsed-out saucepan and bring just to the boil. Pour about half the hot cream into the egg mixture, beating constantly, then pour all this mixture into the saucepan, stirring to blend both mixtures together. Heat just until small bubbles appear around the edge. Add the clarified butter and stir until it melts.

Pour the mixture into a bowl and leave to cool completely, stirring occasionally. Pour in the chilled cream-and-milk mixture and stir until blended. Pour the mixture into an ice cream machine and freeze according to the manufacturer's directions. When it is about three-quarters frozen, stir in the nuts. Alternatively, pour the mixture into a freezerproof container, cover and freeze for 1 hour, or until partially frozen. Remove from the freezer and beat with a fork until smooth. Re-cover and return to the freezer. Repeat the freezing and beating process, then stir in the nuts, return to the freezer and freeze for 1½–2 hours, or until firm. Serve in scoops.

PEACH COBBLER

SERVES 4–6

FILLING

6 peaches, peeled and sliced

4 tbsp caster sugar

$^1/_2$ tbsp lemon juice

$1^1/_2$ tsp cornflour

$^1/_2$ tsp almond or vanilla essence

PIE TOPPING

175 g/6 oz plain flour

115 g/4 oz caster sugar

$1^1/_2$ tsp baking powder

$^1/_2$ tsp salt

85 g/3 oz butter, diced

1 egg

5–6 tbsp milk

Preheat the oven to 220°C/425°F/Gas Mark 7. Put the peaches in a 23-cm/9-inch square ovenproof dish that is also suitable for serving. Add the sugar, lemon juice, cornflour and almond essence and toss together. Bake the peaches in the oven for 20 minutes.

Meanwhile, to make the topping, sift the flour, all but 2 tablespoons of the sugar, the baking powder and salt into a bowl. Rub in the butter with the fingertips until the mixture resembles breadcrumbs. Mix the egg and 5 tablespoons of the milk in a jug, then mix into the dry ingredients with a fork until a soft, sticky dough forms. If the dough seems too dry, stir in the extra tablespoon of milk.

Reduce the oven temperature to 200°C/400°F/Gas Mark 6. Remove the peaches from the oven and drop spoonfuls of the topping over the surface, without smoothing. Sprinkle with the remaining sugar, return to the oven and bake for a further 15 minutes, or until the topping is golden brown and firm – the topping will spread as it cooks. Serve hot or at room temperature.

INDULGE

It's Friday night, the long working week is finally over, and it's time to indulge yourself! Forget about the calories for once and invite your girlfriends around for a gossip over some hot buttered Crumpets, some heartwarming Bread & Butter Pudding or a luxurious Crispy Chocolate Pie.

CRUMPETS

MAKES 10–12

350 g/12 oz plain flour

pinch of salt

15 g/¹/₂ oz fresh yeast

1 tsp caster sugar

400 ml/14 fl oz tepid milk

butter and marmalade, to serve

Place the flour and salt in a mixing bowl and mix together. Blend the fresh yeast with the sugar in a basin and add the milk.

Pour the liquid onto the flour and mix everything together until the batter is smooth, beating the batter thoroughly so that it is light and airy. Cover and leave to rise in a warm place for 1 hour, until well risen.

Stir the batter to knock out any air and check the consistency. If it is too thick, add 1 tablespoon of water (it should look rather gloopy). Leave aside for 10 minutes.

Grease a frying pan and 4 crumpet rings or 7.5-cm/3-inch plain cutters. Place the frying pan over a medium heat and leave to heat up for 2 minutes. Arrange the rings in the pan and spoon in enough batter to come halfway up each ring. Cook over a low heat for 5–6 minutes until small holes begin to appear and the top is starting to dry.

Remove the crumpet rings with a palette knife or an oven glove. Turn the crumpets over (the base should be golden brown) and cook the top for just 1–2 minutes to cook through.

Keep the first batch of crumpets warm while you cook the rest of the batter.

Serve freshly cooked with butter and marmalade or, if you want to serve them later, allow them to cool and reheat in a toaster or by the fire.

RHUBARB CRUMBLE

SERVES 6

FILLING

900 g/2 lb rhubarb
115 g/4 oz caster sugar
grated rind and juice of 1 orange
cream, yogurt or custard, to serve (optional)

CRUMBLE

225 g/8 oz plain or wholemeal flour
115 g/4 oz butter
115 g/4 oz soft brown sugar
1 tsp ground ginger

Preheat the oven to 190°C/375°F/Gas Mark 5.

Cut the rhubarb into 2.5-cm/1-inch lengths and place in a 1.7-litre/3-pint ovenproof dish with the sugar and the orange rind and juice.

Make the crumble by placing the flour in a mixing bowl and rubbing in the butter until the mixture resembles breadcrumbs. Stir in the sugar and the ginger.

Spread the crumble evenly over the fruit and press down lightly using a fork.

Bake in the centre of the oven on a baking tray for 25–30 minutes until the crumble is golden brown.

Serve warm with cream, yogurt or custard, if using.

PECAN BROWNIES

MAKES 20

70 g/2½ oz plain dark chocolate

140 g/5 oz plain flour

¾ tsp bicarbonate of soda

¼ tsp baking powder

225 g/8 oz unsalted butter, plus extra
for greasing

100 g/3½ oz demerara sugar

½ tsp almond essence

1 egg

55 g/2 oz pecans

1 tsp milk

icing sugar, for dusting

Preheat the oven to 180°C/350°F/Gas Mark 4. Grease a large baking sheet and line it with greaseproof paper.

Put the chocolate in a heatproof bowl set over a saucepan of simmering water (a double boiler is ideal) and heat until it is melted. Do not let the bowl touch the water. While the chocolate is melting, sift together the flour, bicarbonate of soda and baking powder in a large bowl.

In a separate bowl, cream together the butter and sugar, then mix in the almond essence and the egg. Remove the chocolate from the heat and stir into the butter mixture. Chop the pecans finely, then add them to the bowl, along with the flour mixture and milk and stir until well combined.

Spoon the mixture into the lined roasting tin and smooth it. Transfer to the oven and cook for 30 minutes, or until firm to the touch (it should still be a little gooey in the middle). Remove from the oven and leave to cool completely. Remove from the roasting tin and cut into 20 squares. Dust with icing sugar and serve.

MARSHMALLOW FLOAT

SERVES 4

225 g/8 oz plain chocolate, broken
into pieces
900 ml/1½ pints milk
3 tbsp caster sugar
8 marshmallows

Finely chop the chocolate with a knife or in a food processor. Do not over-process or the chocolate will melt.

Pour the milk into a saucepan and bring to just below boiling point. Remove the saucepan from the heat and whisk in the sugar and the chocolate.

Pour into warmed mugs or heatproof glasses, top with a marshmallow or two and serve immediately.

DEEP CHOCOLATE CHEESECAKE

SERVES 4–6

BASE

4 tbsp butter, melted, plus extra
for greasing
115 g/4 oz digestive biscuits,
finely crushed
2 tsp unsweetened cocoa powder

CHOCOLATE LAYER

800 g/1 lb 12 oz mascarpone cheese
200 g/7 oz icing sugar, sifted
juice of $^{1}/_{2}$ orange
finely grated rind of 1 orange
175 g/6 oz plain dark chocolate,
melted
2 tbsp brandy
chocolate leaves, to decorate

Grease a 20-cm/8-inch loose-bottomed cake tin.

To make the base, put the crushed biscuits, cocoa powder and melted butter into a large bowl and mix well. Press the biscuit mixture evenly over the base of the prepared tin.

Put the mascarpone cheese and sugar into a bowl and stir in the orange juice and rind. Add the melted chocolate and brandy and mix together until thoroughly combined. Spread the chocolate mixture evenly over the biscuit layer. Cover with clingfilm and chill for at least 4 hours.

Remove the cheesecake from the refrigerator, turn out onto a serving platter and decorate with chocolate leaves. Serve immediately.

BREAD & BUTTER PUDDING

SERVES 4–6

85 g/3 oz butter, softened

6 slices thick white bread

55 g/2 oz mixed fruit
(sultanas, currants and raisins)

25 g/1 oz candied peel

3 large eggs

300 ml/10 fl oz milk

150 ml/5 fl oz double cream

55 g/2 oz caster sugar

whole nutmeg, for grating

1 tbsp demerara sugar

Preheat the oven to 180°C/350°F/Gas Mark 4. Use a little of the butter to grease a 20 x 25-cm/8 x 10-inch baking dish and butter the slices of bread. Cut the bread into quarters and arrange half overlapping in the dish.

Scatter half the fruit and peel over the bread, cover with the remaining bread slices and add the remaining fruit and peel.

In a mixing jug, whisk the eggs well and mix in the milk, cream and caster sugar. Pour this over the pudding and leave to stand for 15 minutes to allow the bread to soak up some of the egg mixture. Tuck in most of the fruit as you don't want it to burn in the oven. Grate the nutmeg over the top of the pudding, according to taste, and sprinkle over the demerara sugar.

Place the pudding on a baking tray and bake at the top of the oven for 30–40 minutes until just set and golden brown.

Remove from the oven and serve warm.

LEMON MERINGUE PIE

SERVES 4

PASTRY

200 g/7 oz plain flour, plus extra
for dusting
100 g/3¹/₂ oz butter, diced, plus extra
for greasing
50 g/1³/₄ oz icing sugar, sifted
finely grated rind of 1 lemon
1 egg yolk, beaten
3 tbsp milk

FILLING

3 tbsp cornflour
300 ml/10 fl oz cold water
juice and grated rind of 2 lemons
175 g/6 oz caster sugar
2 eggs, separated

To make the pastry, sift the flour into a bowl and rub in the butter. Mix in the remaining ingredients. Knead briefly on a lightly floured work surface, then leave to rest for 30 minutes.

Preheat the oven to 180°C/350°F/Gas Mark 4. Grease a 20-cm/8-inch ovenproof pie dish. Roll out the pastry to a thickness of 5 mm/¹/₄ inch and use it to line the dish. Prick with a fork, line with baking paper and fill with baking beans. Bake for 15 minutes. Remove from the oven and discard the baking paper and the baking beans. Reduce the oven temperature to 150°C/300°F/Gas Mark 2.

To make the filling, mix the cornflour with a little water. Put the remaining water into a saucepan. Stir in the lemon juice and rind and cornflour paste. Bring to the boil, stirring. Cook for 2 minutes. Cool a little. Stir in 5 tablespoons of the sugar and the egg yolks, then pour the mixture into the pastry case. In a bowl, whisk the egg whites until stiff. Gradually whisk in the remaining sugar and spread over the pie. Bake for 40 minutes. Remove from the oven and serve.

BANOFFEE PIE

SERVES 4–6

FILLING

800 ml/28 fl oz canned sweetened condensed milk

4 ripe bananas

juice of ¹/₂ lemon

1 tsp vanilla essence

75 g/2³/₄ oz plain chocolate, grated

450 ml/16 fl oz double cream, whipped

BISCUIT BASE

85 g/3 oz butter, melted, plus extra for greasing

150 g/5¹/₂ oz digestive biscuits, crushed into crumbs

50 g/1³/₄ oz shelled almonds, toasted and ground

50 g/1³/₄ oz shelled hazelnuts, toasted and ground

Place the unopened cans of milk in a large saucepan and add enough water to cover them. Bring to the boil, then reduce the heat and simmer for 2 hours, topping up the water level to keep the cans covered. Lift out the hot cans and leave to cool.

Preheat the oven to 180°C/350°F/Gas Mark 4. Grease a 23-cm/9-inch flan tin with butter. Put the remaining butter in a bowl and add the crushed biscuits and ground nuts. Mix together well, then press the mixture evenly into the base and side of the flan tin. Bake for 10–12 minutes, then remove from the oven and leave to cool.

Peel and slice the bananas and put in a bowl. Squeeze over the juice from the lemon, add the vanilla essence and mix together. Spread the banana mixture over the biscuit crust in the tin, then spoon the contents of the cooled cans of condensed milk over the bananas. Sprinkle over 50 g/1³/₄ oz of the chocolate, then top with a layer of whipped cream. Sprinkle over the remaining grated chocolate and serve the pie at room temperature.

STICKY TOFFEE PUDDING

SERVES 4

PUDDING

2 tbsp butter, plus extra for greasing

75 g/2³/₄ oz sultanas

150 g/5¹/₂ oz stoned dates, chopped

1 tsp bicarbonate of soda

200 g/7 oz soft light brown sugar

2 eggs

200 g/7 oz self-raising flour, sifted

STICKY TOFFEE SAUCE

2 tbsp butter

175 ml/6 fl oz double cream

200 g/7 oz soft light brown sugar

Preheat the oven to 180°C/350°F/Gas Mark 4. Grease a 20-cm/8-inch round cake tin.

To make the pudding, put the fruit and bicarbonate of soda into a heatproof bowl. Cover with boiling water and leave to soak. Put the butter into a separate bowl, add the sugar and mix well. Beat in the eggs, then fold in the flour. Drain the soaked fruit, add to the bowl and mix. Spoon the mixture evenly into the prepared cake tin. Transfer to the oven and bake for 35–40 minutes. The pudding is cooked when a skewer inserted into the centre comes out clean.

About 5 minutes before the end of the cooking time, make the sauce. Melt the butter in a saucepan over a medium heat. Stir in the cream and sugar and bring to the boil, stirring constantly. Reduce the heat and simmer for 5 minutes.

Turn out the pudding onto a serving plate and pour over the sauce.

CRISPY CHOCOLATE PIE

SERVES 6

PIE BASE

butter, for greasing

2 egg whites

100 g/3¹/₂ oz ground almonds

4 tbsp ground rice

125 g/4¹/₂ oz caster sugar

¹/₄ tsp almond essence

FILLING

225 g/8 oz plain chocolate, broken
into small pieces

4 egg yolks

4 tbsp icing sugar

4 tbsp whisky

4 tbsp double cream

TO DECORATE

150 ml/5 fl oz whipped cream

55 g/2 oz plain chocolate, grated

Preheat the oven to 160°C/325°F/Gas Mark 3. Grease a 20-cm/8-inch flan tin and line the base with baking paper. Whisk the egg whites in a clean, grease-free bowl until stiff peaks form. Gently fold in the ground almonds, ground rice, caster sugar and almond essence. Spread the mixture over the base and side of the prepared tin. Bake in the preheated oven for 15 minutes.

Meanwhile, to make the filling, place the chocolate in a heatproof bowl set over a saucepan of barely simmering water until melted. Remove from the heat and leave to cool slightly, then beat in the egg yolks, icing sugar, whisky and double cream until thoroughly incorporated.

Remove the flan tin from the oven and pour in the chocolate mixture. Cover with foil, return to the oven and bake at the same temperature for 20–25 minutes until set. Remove from the oven and leave to cool completely.

Cut the pie into 6 slices. Decorate each slice with whipped cream and grated chocolate. Serve immediately.

Index